Chins Up

Chins Up

Your Daily Source of Awesome Energy

by

Josette Dixon Hall

other entities to ensure that we always keep our "Chins Up" with hope, positivity, faith, and self-confidence. May this book offer a daily surge of inspiration to everyone who reads its contents. May God bless every reader.

J

Day 1: Today, do not dwell on the past, and refuse to be anxious about the future. Instead, live in the moment of this day. Relish in the beauty of this gift of life. Accept things for what they are, and deal with them accordingly. Today, choose to be worry-free and at peace, for life, in all its ups and downs, is well worth it.

Day 2: Today is a new day! No matter what you faced yesterday, you survived. Today, you muster the energy needed to conquer this day. Take a moment to admire the beauty in the skies, and the rays of the sunlight. The sun will give you energy. Today will be productive. Today will be a beautiful day!

Day 3: You are worthy. You are beautiful. You are talented. You can do whatever you put your mind to. You will not be discouraged. You will not be complacent. You will love this day to its full potential. It is up to you how this day will be, and today you must choose productivity.

Day 4: "The journey of a thousand miles, begins with a single step." Do not procrastinate. You are one step closer to where you want to be.

Day 5: You are not your circumstances. You are not the wrong that others have done to you. You are not your mistakes, and you are not a victim. Release the spirit of fear, regret, and doubt. Replace them with courage, happiness, and confidence. Today will be a great day.

Day 6: You are in control of your emotions. Do not give anyone else the power to alter your mood. You are responsible for your own happiness.

Day 7: You are worthy. You are deserving of all things good. Do not allow situations to rob you of your confidence. If you believe you can… you will.

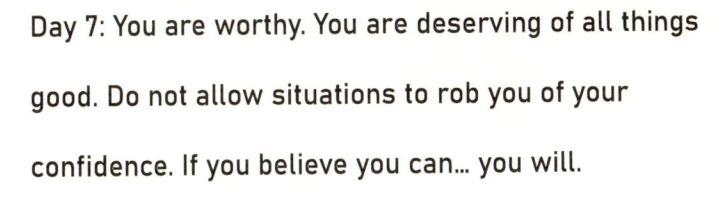

Day 8: Today will be a beautiful day. Focus on all things positive. Detach yourself from anything and anyone that brings negativity. Today will be a beautiful day.

Day 9: Be true to yourself. Be real about your feelings. Do not people--please, instead, please yourself. Make today about you and your peace.

Day 10: It is not where you come from, but it is where you are going that matters. Your history does not define you. Your mistakes do not define you. Your enemies do not define you. Your losses do not define you. Today, make a vow to make steps towards being who you were created to be.

Day 11: Declutter, today. Detach yourself from all meaningless entities and connections.

Day 12: If it compromises your peace, If it brings you pain, If it makes you ashamed, If it does not bring you joy, love, and serenity, then, today, you must free yourself from it.

Day 13: Today, when you look into the mirror, you will see love, you will see beauty, you will see purpose, you will see value, you will see courage, you will see strength, you will see talent, you will see success, you will see hope. Today, when you look into the mirror, you will see your destiny smiling back at you.

Day 14: Depression will not win today. Do not allow unfavorable incidents to set the tone for your entire day. Do not dwell on anything except for positivity. You are human and expected to make mistakes. Today will be beautiful...in spite of...and on purpose.

Day 15: Have a good day today on purpose. Start your day with positiveness. Start your day with love. You are blessed and highly favored. Today will be a beautiful day.

Day 16: Today, the Lord will block all negativity from you. God will guide you. Today, be a blessing to someone else. Today will be filled with light and love.

Day 17: Whatever you should encounter today, know that God will see you through. Thank God in advance. Everything will be okay.

Day 18: Happiness comes from within. Do not look for happiness from your loved ones. Do not depend on happiness from your family and friends. Your job cannot make you happy. The only thing that should control your happiness is you. So, today, give yourself permission to be happy.

Day 19: Some things happen in life that are beyond human control. Declare, today, that if you cannot control it, do not worry about it. The good thing is ...you can control your reaction to it.

Day 20: Self-care is not selfish. Take care of yourself. Putting yourself first is not selfish. You must always take some time to focus on yourself. You matter!

Day 21: There is a dream inside your heart. It will come to fruition. There is a dream inside your soul. It shall be brought to reality. There is a dream that lies in your spirit. You will give birth to it.

Day 22: The Lord will protect you from the wicked. He will deliver you from the pain caused by those you trusted. Do not dwell on your wounds but do dwell on the lessons learned from being hurt, and in turn, spread love and become the best version of yourself.

Day 23: Some days are harder than others. Some days, it is difficult to get out of bed. In those days, look up, and like Lazarus… "Rise and walk!"

Day 24: Depression is real, but so is God. Today, claim blessings and favor. Pray to God to lead you throughout this day. Today will be phenomenal.

Day 25: Just a sliver of light will give you the strength that you need to accomplish your goals today.

Day 26: Do not allow a few seconds of a day to ruin your entire 24 hours. (My Uncle Jimmy shared this with me in a dream.)

Day 27: No matter what you have endured in all of your yesterdays, Today, just as the sun... You will rise and shine.

Day 28: You are the prize. Do not ever forget that!

Day 29: You will find peace in knowing that your loved ones who are absent physically, are still alive in your heart. Love is energy, and energy lives on forever.

Day 30: Forever welcome love, no matter how many times...your heart has been broken. Love is a beautiful thing.

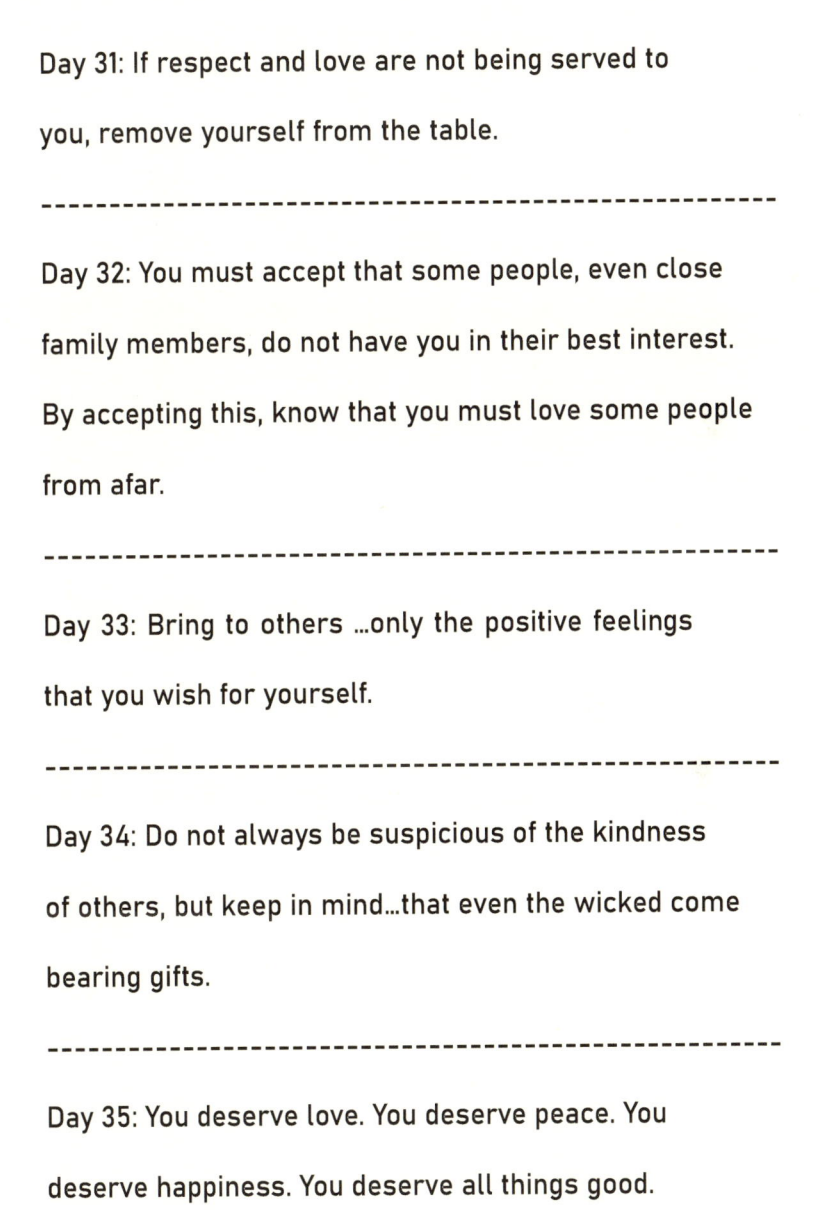

Day 31: If respect and love are not being served to you, remove yourself from the table.

Day 32: You must accept that some people, even close family members, do not have you in their best interest. By accepting this, know that you must love some people from afar.

Day 33: Bring to others …only the positive feelings that you wish for yourself.

Day 34: Do not always be suspicious of the kindness of others, but keep in mind…that even the wicked come bearing gifts.

Day 35: You deserve love. You deserve peace. You deserve happiness. You deserve all things good.

Day 36: When you are tired, rest without guilt.

Day 37: Today, set reasonable goals for yourself, and complete them at your own pace.

Day 38: Rejection is but a detour ... to get you back on the right track.

Day 39: Be kind to everyone, but also, be aware of the fact that not everyone should have access to you.

Day 40: You are more than enough. Believe that!

Day 41: If you believe in yourself, no one else has to. What is already valid, never needs validation.

Day 42: Your life is not written in stone. God has granted you free-will. If you do not like the direction in which your life is going, you have the power to change it, as many times as you can, until it is right with your soul.

Day 43: After darkness comes light. After rain comes the sunshine. After storms come the rainbow. All you have to do is keep going.

Day 44: You do not have to fit in because you were created to stand out. Embrace your uniqueness.

Day 45: Let no one else control your actions.

Day 46: People come, and people go. Those who were meant to be in your life will stay.

Day 47: Realize the fact that expectations lead to disappointment. Therefore, be selective in who you set expectations for.

Day 48: Peace starts from within.

Day 49: What is meant to be... will be, no matter how much you fight it. Whatever is not meant to be, will not be, no matter how much you force it. Pray for guidance to distinguish between the two and know that whatever happens or does not happen...is all in the plan.

Day 50: It is the power within you... that will strengthen you to seek and obtain your desires.

Day 51: You are who you are. People can accept you as you are or lose out on that which is good!

Day 52: Do not apologize for who you are. You are greatness!

Day 53: You are royalty, and God's kingdom is your palace.

Day 54: Play to win. Otherwise, what is the point of being in the game?

Day 55: God did not create you to succumb to mediocrity. You are destined for greatness.

Day 56: There are lessons in every mistake; learning from them lightens the load, makes you wiser, and, ultimately, makes you a better person.

Day 57: Today, pray for the spirit of discernment.

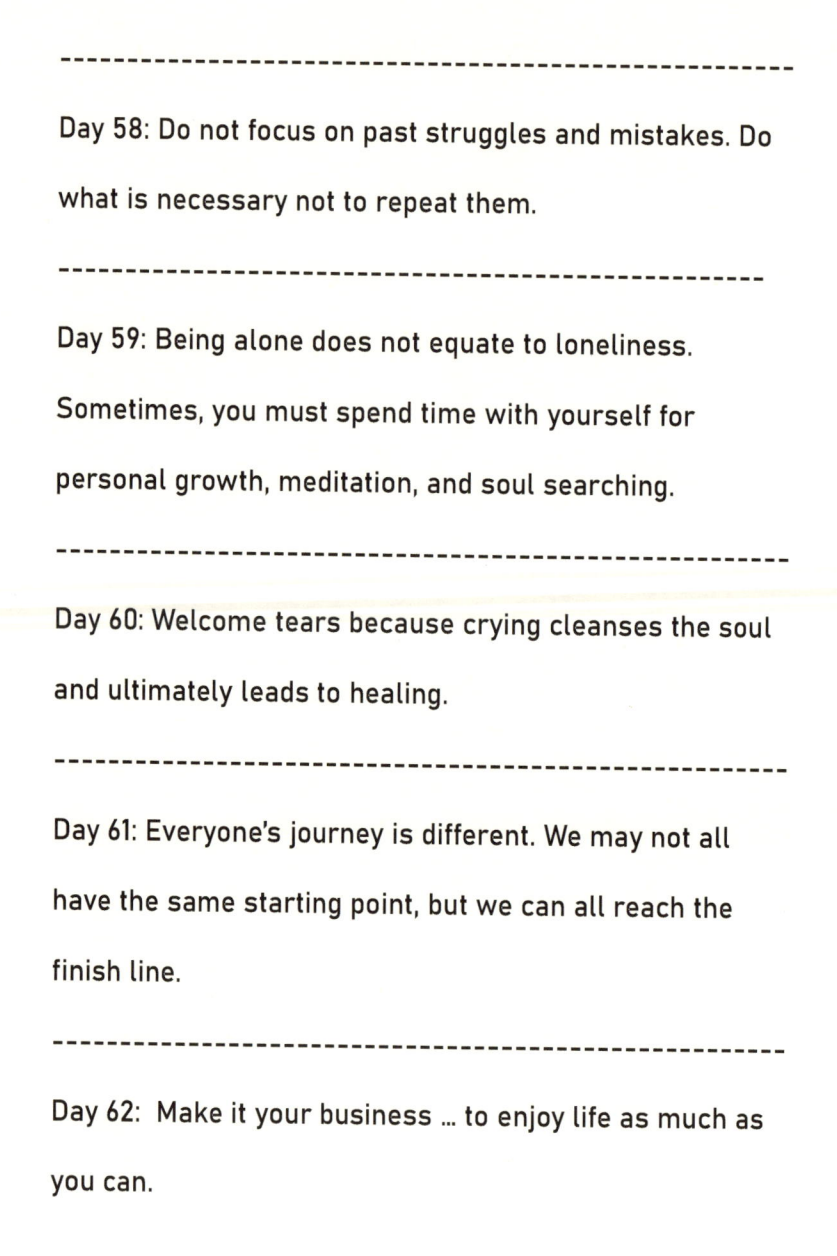

Day 58: Do not focus on past struggles and mistakes. Do what is necessary not to repeat them.

Day 59: Being alone does not equate to loneliness. Sometimes, you must spend time with yourself for personal growth, meditation, and soul searching.

Day 60: Welcome tears because crying cleanses the soul and ultimately leads to healing.

Day 61: Everyone's journey is different. We may not all have the same starting point, but we can all reach the finish line.

Day 62: Make it your business ... to enjoy life as much as you can.

Day 63: Tough times are inevitable in life, but the good thing is …they are only temporary.

Day 64: Life is not forever. So, make the best of each day.

Day 65: God will fight your battles.

Day 66: Life is always, always worth living.

Day 67: There is no limit to the times that you can…refocus and restart.

Day 68: To get the chance to start over at square one is a blessing.

Day 69: If you do not have the ability to change it, then it is not your place to worry about it.

Day 70: Pray and do your part in improving situations because worrying is a waste of precious time.

Day 71: You deserve the best in life. Go for it.

Day 72: You are blessed beyond measure.

Day 73: Every day is a new day to right a wrong, a new day to start fresh, a new day of hope, of aspiration, and of love.

Day 74: Today, bless someone. A simple compliment, a warm smile, an endearing hug…a good deed can go a long way.

Day 75: Clarity comes in the wee hours … when all is still.

Day 76: If it is not in your heart, then do not do it. Your actions should be purpose driven.

Day 77: Your body... Is your temple. Be careful what you allow to enter into it.

Day 78: It is human nature to desire love. However, do not look for it, but rather... allow it to find you.

Day 79: God has given you discernment It is also known as your "gut instinct." Always allow it to guide you.

Day 80: It is okay to ask questions, but better to watch actions. Motives and answers are always found in behavior.

Day 81: Do not take everything personally. Often times, people's attitudes and actions are about their personal struggles. Do not allow someone else's attitude or action to dictate your behavior.

Day 82: Love does not hurt. Love does not neglect. Love does not disrespect. Love eases pain, comforts, and appreciates.

Day 83: Do not complain about your frustrations, instead… rejoice in all the ways you are and have been blessed.

Day 84: Have no worries. God will guide you.

Day 85: The first steps to healing of any kind…is accepting the fact that there is an issue. Ignoring adversities do not make them go away, but it does block the healing process.

Day 86: Jesus loves you! Remember this!

Day 87: Success comes only to those who work for it.

Day 88: Love is an ACTION verb. If love does not appear in one's actions...it does not exist.

Day 89: Today, give it to God... your fears, your worries, your desires, your prayers, your goals. Whatever it is, give it to God.

Day 90: Of all the gifts in the world, life is the most precious. Appreciate it by making the best of it.

Day 91: Time cannot be recycled. Use your time wisely.

Day 92: God is your guiding light. Do not fear dark times. He will lead you.

Day 93: It is okay to love ... again, and again and again.

Day 94: In due season...Your hard work will pay off.

Day 95: Do not give up during the process. Persistence is key.

Day 96: Not many people will like you. Even fewer will love you, being perfectly okay with this will bring you peace.

Day 97: There is a difference between standards and preferences. Always maintain your standards. While at the same time, make sure that your preferences do not lead to self-restriction.

Day 98: Others will learn how to treat you. based on what you accept and what you refuse to accept.

Day 99: Be there for others, but not at the expense of your own peace and happiness.

Day 100: If it is meant to be, it will be…At times, the journey will be effortlessly and painlessly. At other times, it will not…But if it is meant for you, no one can stop it.

Day 101: You can only expect people to be themselves. Expecting anything else, without a doubt, will lead to disappointment.

Day 102: Always be true to yourself. You can run from your feelings, but you cannot hide.

Day 103: Prayer along with faith diminishes worry.

Day 104: Just because time changes, it does not always mean that people do.

Day 105: Liberation can be found... in expressing your feelings in an uncensored fashion.

Day 106: It is impossible to save the world, but it is mandatory to save yourself.

Day 107: Temporary people ... should not be given permanent privileges in your life.

Day 108: It is okay to say "no." Sometimes, in order to save yourself, you must learn to say "no."

Day 109: If your heart and mind should ever disagree, then choose to follow your soul.

Day 110: Energy never lies.

Day 111: Do not respond to negative remarks made against you. Do not respond to anyone that purposely tries to annoy you. Do not respond to anything that has no merit. Do not respond to foolishness or ignorance. Because in many cases, silence speaks volumes.

Day 112: God always knows what is best for you. So, if something never seems to work out, no matter how hard you try, know that it is God redirecting you.

Day 113: As they say in In-flight: "Put on your oxygen mask first, before aiding someone else in putting on theirs."

Day 114: No matter what lies are being told on you, no matter how anyone tries to scandalize your name, you do not have to say a word because the light from within you will always prove them wrong.

Day 115: God's acceptance… is all the acceptance that you will ever need.

Day 116: Inner beauty never fades.

Day 117: Material things can be nice, but they do not make or break you. You are not your car. You are not your house. You are not your clothing. Whatever you choose to drive, wherever you choose to live, whatever you choose to wear do not dictate your salvation.

Day 118: You have a right to end anything that compromises your peace: A job, A relationship, A friendship, A goal, Letting go of that which compromises your peace and sanity does not make you a quitter. It makes you wise.

Day 119: Today, pray that God will order your steps. He will guide you to where he intends for you to be. He will watch over you and your loved ones. God will keep the wicked far away from you. He will place His angels around you for protection. Today, pray that God will order your steps.

Day 120: In those times in which you are confused, be still and pray. Wait upon the Lord, and He shall be your guide.

Day 121: Do not waste time counting the days. Instead, be productive and make the days count.

Day 122: The love of God and the love of self will set the pace for you to love others and for others to love you.

Day 123: Start each day in expectancy of God's blessings, of God's goodness, of God's grace.

Day 124: The road that you are on today, is a result of your past choices. The road that you will meet tomorrow will be the result of the choices that you make today. Pray for discernment, courage, and wisdom to make choices that will lead you to the road to your destiny.

Day 125: Be grateful for all your life's experiences. Unfavorable encounters teach you lessons. The better happenings enrich your world. Good or bad, rain or shine, Life is so worth it!

Day 126: Do not be anxious. Just pray.

Day 127: If there is breath in your body, you have the opportunity...to right a wrong, to ask for forgiveness, to love somebody, to live your dreams...As long as there is breath in your body, you can do whatever He wills.

Day 128: Be mindful that wisdom is a fruit that does

not sprout on every tree. It does not automatically come with age. Education does not guarantee it. It cannot be imitated. Do not assume that one is wise just because one is aged.

Day 129: Do not be so quick to try and explain everything to everybody. People can only understand at their own levels of comprehension, and there are many with preconceived notions and narrow minds. Everyone will not get you or understand you, and you must find peace in being okay with it.

Day 130: Do something daily that makes you happy.

Day 131: Look inside yourself...Sometimes for the root of the problem...always for the solution.

Day 132: Prayer should be daily. Whether times are good or bad... You must go to God, first, with thanksgiving.

You must have faith and believe that whatever you ask of God, you shall receive.

Day 133: Mental health and physical health are equally important. A strong mind and a strong body are essential in living life to your fullest potential.

Day 134: When people cross you once, it is their fault. If you give them a second chance, you gamble. A third time ...you are a part of the problem. In essence, people can only continue to do wrong against you if you allow it.

Day 135: Check lists serve as great visual organizers when setting both short term and long-term goals and aspirations.

Day 136: Whatever you give in secret to those in need... God will certainly "reward you openly."

Day 137: Respect the fact that your intuition is your soul...it will speak to you in times of uncertainty. Learn to listen to it.

Day 138: Real friends are there during... the sunshine. and the rain.

Day 139: When God calls you to do something, It is up to you to do it, whether you have support from others or not.

Day 140: Just like the sun, you must arise every morning, and allow your light to shine.

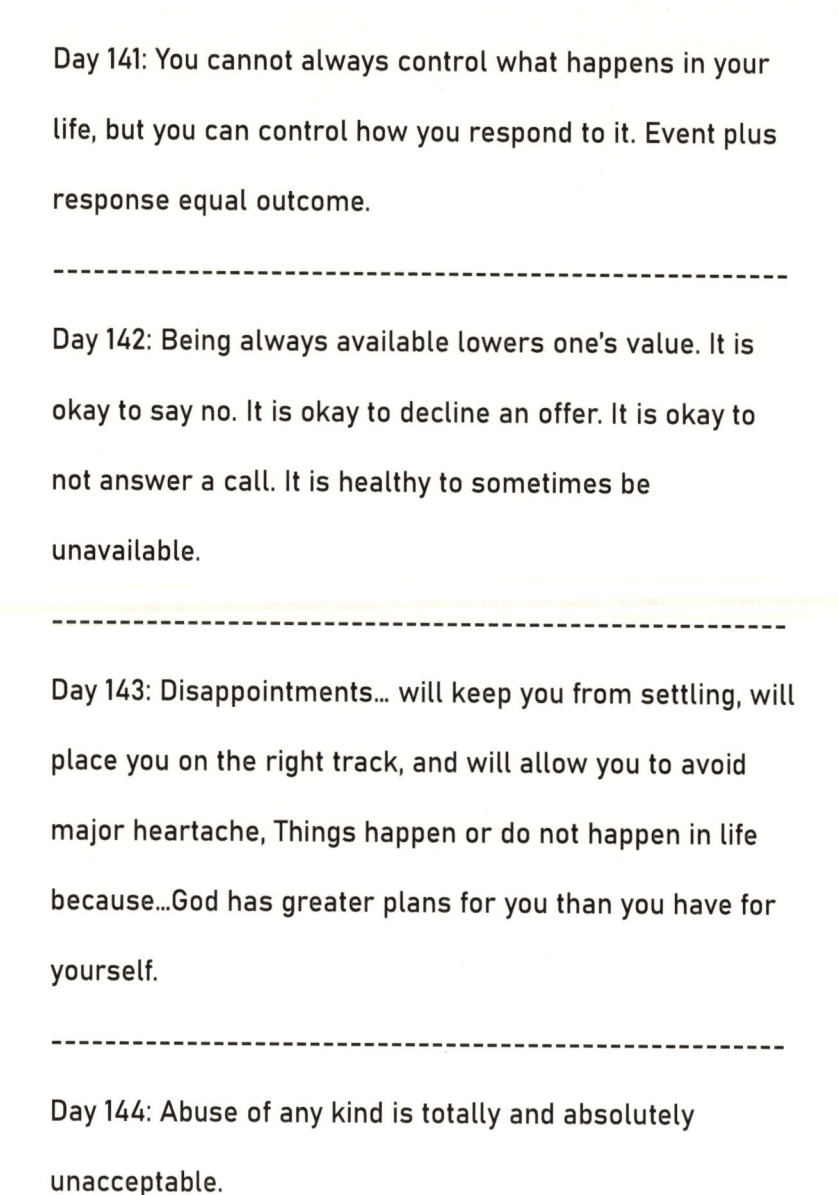

Day 141: You cannot always control what happens in your life, but you can control how you respond to it. Event plus response equal outcome.

Day 142: Being always available lowers one's value. It is okay to say no. It is okay to decline an offer. It is okay to not answer a call. It is healthy to sometimes be unavailable.

Day 143: Disappointments... will keep you from settling, will place you on the right track, and will allow you to avoid major heartache, Things happen or do not happen in life because...God has greater plans for you than you have for yourself.

Day 144: Abuse of any kind is totally and absolutely unacceptable.

Day 145: Overindulgence in anything is unhealthy.

Day 146: The key to success is to keep moving… despite obstacles, despite fear, despite naysayers, and despite self-doubt.

Day 147: All that you are and all that you dare to be… is not because you are lucky, but it is because you are blessed.

Day 148: "Hope, faith, and love, but… the greatest of these is love." 1 Corinthians 13 v 13

Day 149: Desires and needs are not always one in the same. You must distinguish between the two and act accordingly.

Day 150: Success is the result of desire, hard work, talent, skills, and the strength and courage to keep it moving, even when goals seem unattainable.

Day 151: Choose your words carefully, because once they are spoken, they cannot be undone. Cruel words cause pain, kind words soothe.

Day 152: Never chase people. Chase goals, chase dreams, and ultimately... chase salvation.

Day 153: Bad habits must be acknowledged. before they can be broken. Some things and people offer temporary gratification.... but long-term negative effects.

Day 154: Being grateful, appreciating, and taking care of what you have open the doors to abundance.

Day 155: Anyone that complains about your standards being too high... are simply too low for you to be dealing with.

Day 156: Whatever it is, God can heal it. Just pray and believe.

Day 157: Every relationship has its issues. No one is perfect. You just have to determine whose flaws you are willing to deal with, and at the same time, make sure the love and respect are mutual.

Day 158: Stop allowing society to make your decisions for you.

Day 159: You must separate yourself from toxic and hateful people. If you do not, you could end up hating them, and hating another person is self-destructive.

Day 160: Envious people want what you have. Jealous people hate who you are. Do not allow either of them to stop your hustle or dim your light.

Day 161: A happy life is not all work. A fruitful life is not all play. However, the best life can be created… with a sufficient balance between the two.

Day 162: Today is a good day for a random act of kindness. You never know when you are "entertaining an angel."

Day 163: Do not be afraid of change, for change is necessary for growth.

Day 164: Some things you just must charge to the game, keep it moving, and never look back.

Day 165: Forgiving those who hurt you is necessary... for you to move on.

Day 166: When you get what you have prayed for, appreciate it, enjoy it, and take care of it. Because if you neglect it, you may find yourself praying for it again.

Day 167: You cannot base things on the opinions of others. Experience things for yourself. Everyone is wired differently. The same thing that someone else complains about, could be all that you ever dreamed of.

Day 168: Believe in your abilities. Believe in your talents. Believe in your special gifts. Believe in your dreams. Always, believe in yourself.

Day 169: Genuine beauty has more to do with your heart.

than your physical appearance.

Day 170: The popular route is not necessarily the

better route. Do not do it because everyone else is doing

it. Do not do it because others expect you to do it.

Do it because it sits well with your soul...

Day 171: Be sure to pray today and every day. Pray not only

in times of need. Pray also to give thanks to God for all of

your blessings.

Day 172: Never compare yourself to anyone else.

Day 173: Peace...true peacefulness... is found when you

have no need to prove anything to anybody.

Day 174: Life is a journey. Our experiences break us, mend us, and ultimately, shape us into who we are meant to become.

Day 175: Enemies are but twisted fans. Never let them get you down.

Day 176: Nothing is more uplifting than a good laugh! Laughter is contagious. Laughter brings joy. Laughter nourishes the soul.

Day 177: Have you spent time with God today? Pray. Read a few scriptures. Reflect upon His word. You will be glad you did.

Day 178: Having a true friend requires being a true friend.

Day 179: As you elevate in life... not everyone will clap, but it is okay.... elevate anyway.

Day 180: Life is not a competition. Do your own thing, at your own pace. With determination and a strong work ethic, you will get there.

Day 181: Sometimes, the reason you do not receive what you are praying for is because...You are not prepared for it. Your mindset may not be able to handle it. You may have the wrong people in your life. You still have a few lessons to learn. However, you will receive it when the time is right, for God is always an on-time God.

Day 182: Learn to accept and respect God's "No."

Day 183: Do not base your self-worth on... the opinions of others, material things, or losses. Your self-worth is priceless. because you are rare and incomparable.

Day 184: Do not wait for opportunities... create them.

Day 185: Sometimes, it is not that you need to change your mind, but instead, you need to train your mind.

Day 186: There are twenty-four hours in a single day. If managed wisely, it is amazing what you can accomplish.

Day 187: Constant failure in the same situation is... redirection.

Day 188: Be patient. Things will happen when they are supposed to.

Day 189: Your character introduces you... before you introduce yourself. Make an authentic and exceptional first impression.

Day 190: Be positive, even during periods of uncertainty. A positive mindset attracts positive outcomes. Optimism is powerful.

Day 191: Communicate. Never expect for anyone... to assume how you feel, tell them and show them.

Day 192: Most of your strength will come from ...times of adversity. Difficult times in life are inevitable, but when you learn the lessons that they present, you will become stronger and wiser.

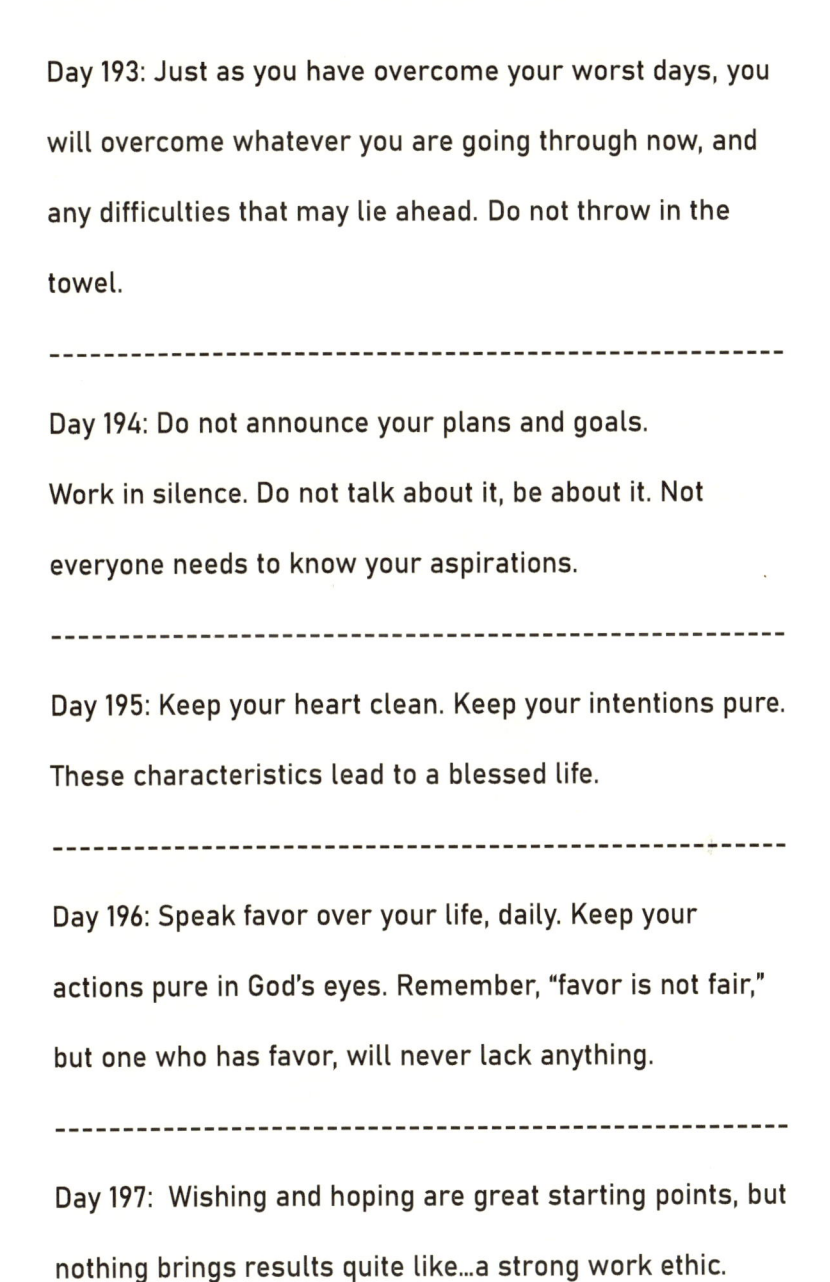

Day 193: Just as you have overcome your worst days, you will overcome whatever you are going through now, and any difficulties that may lie ahead. Do not throw in the towel.

Day 194: Do not announce your plans and goals. Work in silence. Do not talk about it, be about it. Not everyone needs to know your aspirations.

Day 195: Keep your heart clean. Keep your intentions pure. These characteristics lead to a blessed life.

Day 196: Speak favor over your life, daily. Keep your actions pure in God's eyes. Remember, "favor is not fair," but one who has favor, will never lack anything.

Day 197: Wishing and hoping are great starting points, but nothing brings results quite like…a strong work ethic.

Day 198: Be not afraid. You can overcome the spirit of frightfulness… by facing your fears.

Day 199: Live life as if tomorrow may never come because one day it will not. Love your loved ones like you will never see them again because, one day, you will not. Do not take the power of today for granted, for "tomorrow is not promised."

Day 200: You've got this. Do not give up on your dreams. If there is breath in your body, there is purpose in your life.

Day 201: Everyone has room for improvement, but as you make the necessary changes to become the best version of "you," embrace yourself, love yourself, and be proud of who you are.

Day 202: Open minds open doors.

Day 203: Never settle for anything. If your heart is not in it... you should not be either.

Day 204: Choose the option that is best... for you.

Day 205: Sometimes, you have to hug yourself, and that can be a good thing. Self-love.... Self-care.

Day 206: Be self-sufficient, but welcome support and love that come from a good place.

Day 207: When you are your greatest cheerleader... you cannot lose.

Day 208: Be excited about life. Be excited about love. Be excited about your goals. Be excited about new plans. Be excited about the future. Be excited, and always stand in expectancy for great things.

Day 209: Dream...wide awake.

Day 210: One who remains loyal to disloyal people... robs himself of respect.

Day 211: Always take responsibility for your actions.

Day 212: Plant yourself in peace, persistence, and positivity...and watch yourself bloom into prosperity.

Day 213: Believe in yourself. Believe in your abilities. Believe in your talents. Believe in your dreams. Never doubt yourself. "You can do all things through Christ, who strengthens you."

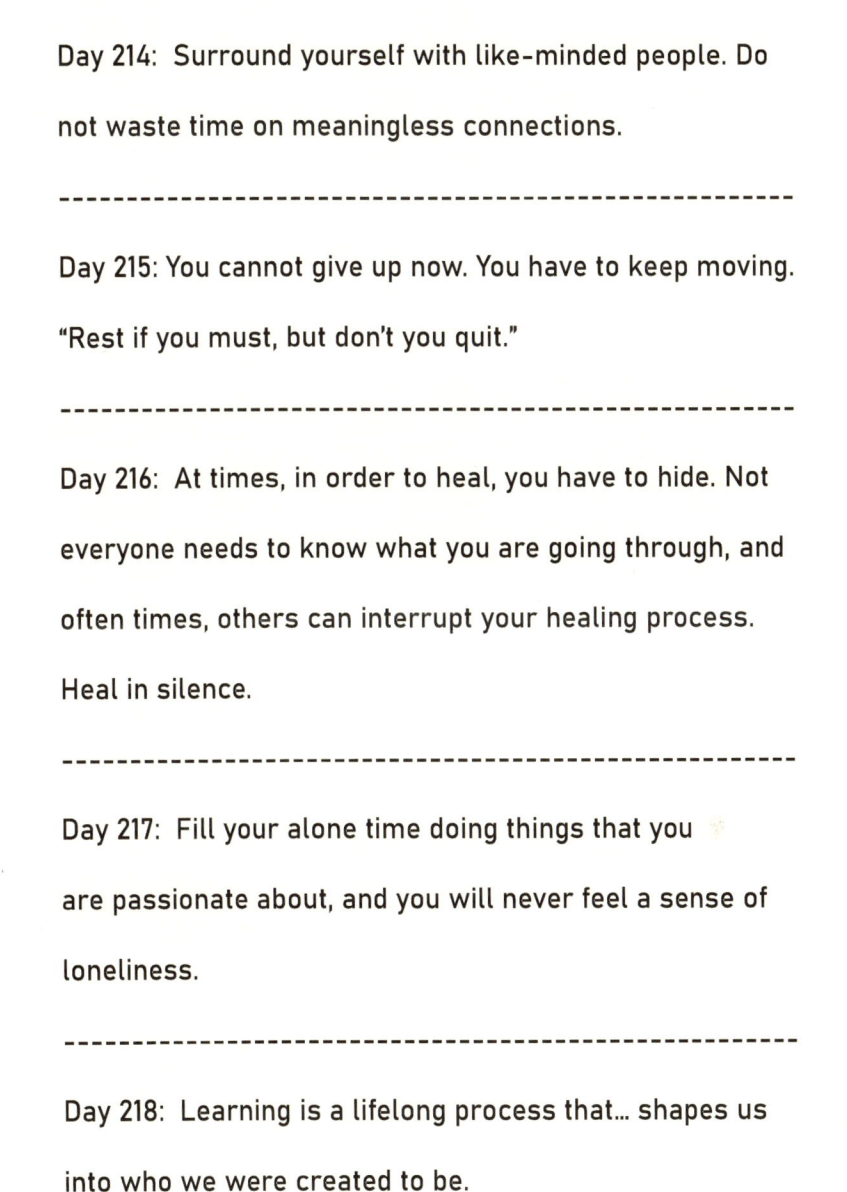

Day 214: Surround yourself with like-minded people. Do not waste time on meaningless connections.

Day 215: You cannot give up now. You have to keep moving. "Rest if you must, but don't you quit."

Day 216: At times, in order to heal, you have to hide. Not everyone needs to know what you are going through, and often times, others can interrupt your healing process. Heal in silence.

Day 217: Fill your alone time doing things that you are passionate about, and you will never feel a sense of loneliness.

Day 218: Learning is a lifelong process that... shapes us into who we were created to be.

Day 219: Do not place limitations on yourself...You are not too old. You are not too young. You are not weak. You are strong enough. You are smart enough. Free your mind of limitations, and soar into new heights.

Day 220: Everyone has a gift. Search your soul to see where your talent lies. That which comes naturally and frees your mind...Is your gift from God.

Day 221: Visualize it. Write it down. Create a plan. Check the steps off as you go. These are ingredients for successfully completing your goals.

Day 222: A heart of gratitude opens the door... Tomori abundance. Be grateful for what you have and watch as your blessings multiply.

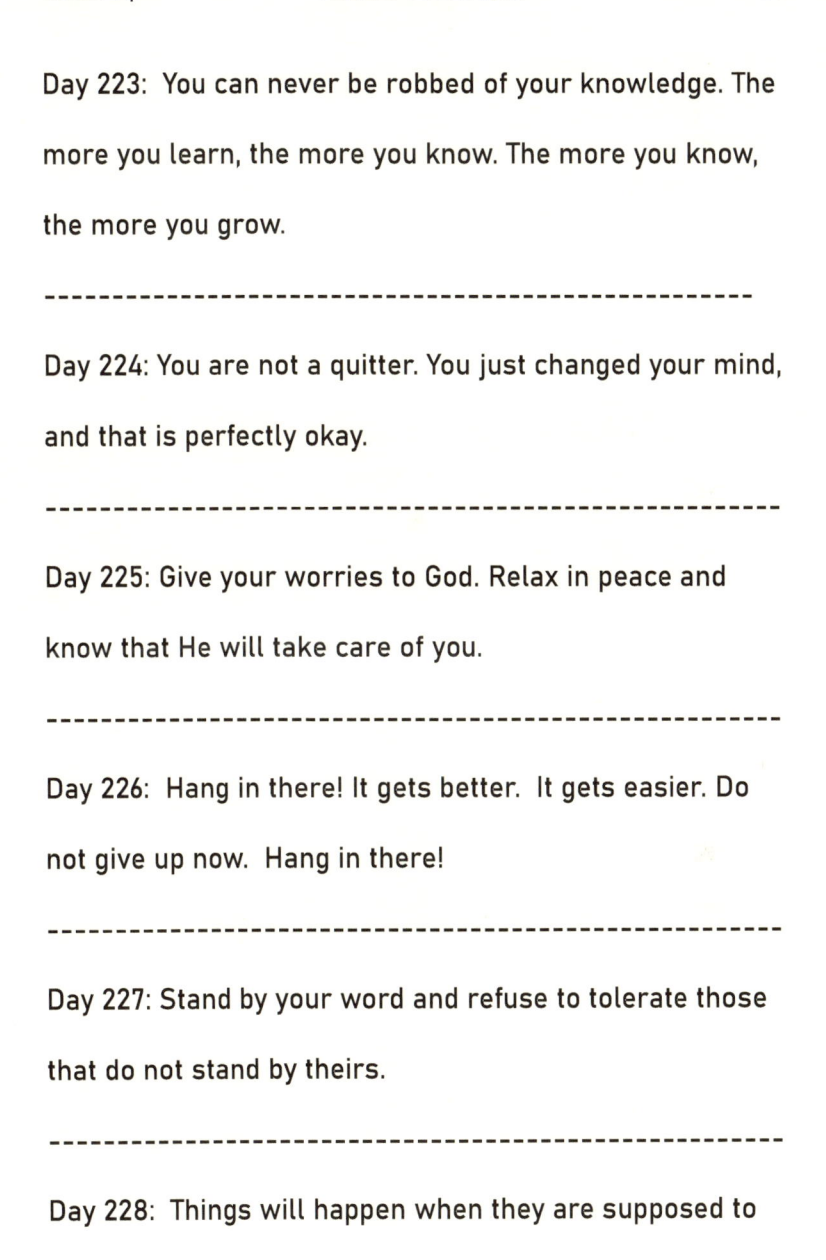

Day 223: You can never be robbed of your knowledge. The more you learn, the more you know. The more you know, the more you grow.

Day 224: You are not a quitter. You just changed your mind, and that is perfectly okay.

Day 225: Give your worries to God. Relax in peace and know that He will take care of you.

Day 226: Hang in there! It gets better. It gets easier. Do not give up now. Hang in there!

Day 227: Stand by your word and refuse to tolerate those that do not stand by theirs.

Day 228: Things will happen when they are supposed to

happen. Your plans will sometimes be interrupted, but if situations are meant to be, they will be… at the right time.

Day 229: You are one step closer to where you want to be. Do not give up. Keep going.

Day 230: When life gets hard… pray harder.

Day 231: Sometimes, you just have to be still. In stillness, you will find peace, you will find clarity, and you will comfort.

Day 232: Respect yourself and respect others.

Day 223: When people treat you badly, it is a reflection of themselves, not a reflection of you.

Day 234: Do not make those a priority in your life… when

they are too busy for you. No one is "too busy." People make time for what and who they prioritize.

Day 235: Do not feel guilty about letting go… of toxic people, people who compromise your peace, and people who disregard your "no."

Day 236: There is no need to "rush" into a relationship. Those who "rush" into relationships have motives. Take your time and really… get to know people.

Day 237: Be careful… who you allow into your home, who you allow into your heart, and who you allow into your life. Not everyone has good intentions, and demonic transferring is real.

Day 238: There is a major difference between an associate and a friend. An associate is with you based on situations; a friend is with you based on love.

Day 239: Take care of your needs.

Day 240: Rewind, relax, reset… as often as you need to.

Day 241: When God puts an idea into your mind and your heart, you must carry it through…and He will guide you every step of the way.

Day 242: Sometimes, you must unlearn the toxic things… that you were taught as a child.

Day 243: Think only positive thoughts today. Optimism is powerful.

Day 244: Today, decide that you will have a great day…and you will.

Day 245: Not everything and everyone presented to you is an opportunity. Sometimes, they are distractions. Pray for guidance and discernment to distinguish between the two.

Day 246: You meet everyone for a reason. Some will teach you a lesson. Some will provide information. Some will bring you comfort. Others will bring you love, but not everyone is meant to stay in your life. So, when their objectives have been met, and it is time for them to depart…let them go.

Day 247: Your attitude in life…. will contribute much to your altitude in life.

Day 248: Smile a lot, even when you do not feel like it. Eventually, smiling will boost your mood. It is a proven fact.

Day 249: Do nothing just for the sake of appearances and be cautious of those who do. If it is not coming from your heart, do not do it. Fake people do that.

Day 250: Nature is God's art... created to add upliftment and beauty to the world. Relish its beauty and witness your spirit glow.

Day 251: You are stronger than you believe you are.

Day 252: If it feels good to your soul... If it soothes your soul... If it sets right with your soul...By all means, do it...it is meant to be.

Day 253: Wisdom is the result... of learning from mistakes, of overcoming heartache, of getting it wrong sometimes, and of never backing down from that in which you believe.

Day 254: Somebody... somewhere... is praying for someone... like you.

Day 255: Stop stressing over things. Pray...take necessary action...if possible... and leave your worries at the altar. Stressing over things is a waste of time, and it is very unhealthy.

Day 256: Forgiving someone is great... but sometimes, you must also deny access. No access. No return.

Day 257: Get ready...get ready...get ready for...New Beginnings!

Day 258: You are...loved, brave, courageous, brilliant, worthy, and all that good stuff. You are chosen.

Day 259: Do not hold on to pain. Cry if you must. Be true to yourself about your feelings. Never try and flee from your emotions. Let go of the pain, heal, and move on.

Day 260: The only acceptance you need in this world is…God's.

Day 261: In some situations, you have to place your focus on yourself, and allow other things to just play out. What is meant to happen…will happen.

Day 262: It is great to be a part of a positive place of worship, to fellowship with others and hear the word of God. Be careful, though, not to become so wrapped up… in the building and its people… for the church…the real church is inside your heart.

Day 263: Here is to winning, in advance, in everything that's inside your heart to do. Now go out and win!

Day 264: Ask yourself if you tried hard enough? If so, accept the results. If not, try harder.

Day 265: A quick fix is temporary… instead, discover a solution to issues at hand.

Day 266: Hold on! Life gets better! Don't dare give up!

Day 267: In case no one told you today… you and your life matter.

Day 268: There are no small blessings. Be gracious to God for all things good.

Day 269: Do not wallow in regret. Ask for forgiveness and learn from ... your mistakes and misdeeds.

Day 270: You have to look out for your best interest. If you do not... you cannot expect anyone else to.

Day 271: Use common sense even when rendering kindness. Some people mistake kindness for weakness... and leeches do not discriminate.

Day 272: The mind is very powerful. If you believe you can, you will. Be mindful of what you feed your mind. Always nourish it with positive thoughts.

Day 273: Do not be discouraged by the road ahead of you, but be empowered by how far you have traveled to get to where you are.

Day 274: Every huge success starts off with small steps. Get started now! Do not procrastinate.

Day 275: Possibilities are endless when you create them. Do not waste time waiting for something to happen. Make it happen. You hold the cards. Play to win.

Day 276: Never beg for... affection, attention, association, or anything. If it is not given freely, then it is not worth having.

Day 277: If it brings you peace after you part with it... whatever it may be... you did not lose it, you let it go... and your soul is at peace.

Day 278: Do not just exist... live life to the full.

Day 279: Sometimes, you do not have what you want...because you really do not know what you want. Make the decision that is best for you...and go with it.

Day 280: So many people miss out on the good life... because they are so worried about the opinions of others. Do not allow the judgments of others to cause you to miss out on what makes you happy.

Day 281: The world does revolve around you...if you allow it to. Go for what you want with all that you have.

Day 282: Never stop believing...in God, in your wishes, in your dreams, in your talent, in your abilities. Never stop believing in...yourself.

Day 283: Never lose sleep...over anything that you do not

have control over, over anyone that disrespects you, or over the problems of others.

Day 284: Many people will think your self-confidence is conceit. That is their problem, not yours. Never dumb-down. Never dim your light. Remain balanced and keep being who you are.

Day 285: Today will be a great day. Something great is going to happen. Believe and watch in wonder.

Day 286: God is real. Take some time to communicate with Him daily. Start your prayers off by giving thanks for His blessings. The more you communicate with God… the less you will worry, and your life will become more peaceful.

Day 287: No matter what you are facing today, just know that every situation is temporary. You will survive. You will conquer. Life will go on.

Day 288: What is for you is for you. You will receive what is for you... Even if it is against all odds.

Day 289: No one is perfect. Do not be so critical of yourself, and refrain from being judgmental of others.

Day 290: You must have patience. Even God, who has all power, did not create the world and all of its wonders in one day. Patience prevents anxiety and confusion. Pray, do your part, and be still.

Day 291: When you ask God to order your steps, you are going to wonder why some things did not work out. You are going to wonder why some people left. You are going to wonder why you had to walk away from some people and some places. You may experience some minor disappointments and pain, but in the end…you will be amazed at where God will guide you. Today, ask God to order your steps, and prepare to be elated and elevated.

Day 292: Your true friends are blessings. So, instead of wondering why someone is your enemy, focus on your friends. Be grateful for the gift of friendship. Your true friends may be few in numbers, but they are plentiful in love.

Day 293: You do not have to wonder where you stand will real people. They will both show you and tell you.

Day 294: A little humor goes a long way. Learn to laugh. Being too serious and uptight all the time is not good. Laugh. Make others laugh. Laughter is food for the soul.

Day 295: Stand up straight and communicate with eye contact. Say what you mean and mean what you say, in a tactful manner. Stand by your word and your promises. These characteristics exude confidence and demand respect.

Day 296: Telling the truth will not always make you well-liked by man, but being truthful makes God smile. Who do you serve? God or man? Be truthful and be free.

Day 297: If you do not like it, do not settle for it. If you do not want it, do not settle for it. If it compromises your standards, do not settle for it. If it brings you shame, do not settle for it. By settling for anything less than you deserve, you rob yourself of happiness.

Day 298: Know that everyone's word does not exude honesty, but their truth will reveal itself in their actions. Be watchful.

Day 299: Avoid one-sided connections. If it does not benefit you in anyway, whether intrinsically or extrinsically...Flee far away from it.

Day 300: "Joy always comes in the morning." Not all days will bring sunshine, and many nights there will be rain. Hold on! Better days are ahead. Pray. Joy will come with the rising of the sun.

Day 301: What are you passionate about? Your answer indicates your gift. Use it.

Day 302: Be mindful of the seeds you plant, for that which is planted...with no doubt...will return to you. This is one of the most certain things in life.

Day 303: Being original and authentic...is an epic vibe. Be proud of who you are. Be yourself.

Day 304: Today is a great day... to do that thing that you have been putting off. There is no better time than the present. Do it while you can.

Day 305: Learn to set expectations of people based on who they have proven to be. Expecting anything more of them ...will set you up...to be let down.

Day 306: Heartache is the worst pain, but once you heal from it, there is an upside. No one wants a broken heart but know that after the pain... a new normal awaits. You will be wiser, stronger, and ready for love again.

Day 307: Take the time to see the beauty of one's soul. If the inner man is unsightly, the outer man perishes.

Day 308: You must dig deeper than the surface when in search of treasures. Pebbles are plentiful. Diamonds are rare.

Day 309: Life is an adventure...Do not be afraid to take risks. Challenge yourself to always try something new.

Day 310: If you should find yourself running in circles, then it is high time to step outside of the box.

Day 311: One cannot get a breakthrough... without first going through...Stepping outside of your comfort zone will be uncomfortable at first, but well worth it in the end.

Day 312: Your superpower...is your willpower! How bad do you want it? What are you willing to do to get it?
If it is not an ill-deed...Your willpower will take you there.

Day 313: A calm approach serves in a useful way. It produces positive outcomes. Calm yourself before taking action.

Day 314: Love is...A cool drink on a hot summer day
A sliver of sunshine after clouds of gray. A cool breeze in the month of May. A beacon of light to set you on your way. Love is...

Day 315: Stay focused on your goals. Stay focused on your health. Stay focused on God. Stay focused on everything that matters to you, and your time will never be wasted.

Day 316: Show your loved ones love while they are still alive. Say kind things to your associates while breath is still in their bodies. For when they have departed this earth, it will be too late.

Day 317: Desperation is never a good look, specifically, when it comes to dating and relationships. Do not accept anything from anybody just to have a body next to you. You are worthy of so much more.

Day 318: Marriage and relationships between two people who have mutual love and trust is a beautiful thing. All days together will not be good days. There will be sunshine. There will be rain. Even storms will come, but taking a vow to stay together, to love each other, to have one another's back, and to adhere to those vows within reason, love...love will keep you together... and love is all worthwhile.

Day 319:

Pray for discernment to distinguish between the wolf and the sheep. It's a lot of that going on these days. While some people have good intentions, most people have motives. As the bible states, "Men will become lovers of themselves." In laymen's terms, we live in a dog-eat-dog world. Pray and observe.

Day 320: Be appreciative of what someone willingly does for you. You never know what they went through to make it happen. Do not always base things on size or monetary value. The things you consider little are, often times, the things that mean a lot.

Day 321: Yes, you can do it. Do not doubt yourself or your abilities. If it is what you want, and pleasant in the eyes of God, yes, you can, and yes you will.

Day 322: You will get what you are praying for. You will get what you are wishing for. You will get what you are hoping for...in due season.

Day 323: Today, expect great things! Do not wait for them to happen, make them happen. You have the power to create the life that you want.

Day 324: Be still at times, but never be idle. Being still brings peace and clarity, while idleness produces nothingness.

Day 325: Claim victory today in all that you do. On your mark, get set...go!

Day 326: Do not allow distractions to hinder you from what you know you are created to do.

Day 327: Sometimes people are removed from your Life so that you can focus on what really matters.

Day 328: The best thing that you can do in memory of your loved ones who have gone on to the spirit world is to be the best that you can be. Go ahead. Make your angels smile.

Day 329: Go and get it! You've got gusto, so what are you waiting for?

Day 330: God has brought you from a long way, and He will continue to carry you. Keep the faith!

Day 331: Every spoken word, and every moment of action...create memories. Make them unforgettable.

Day 332: If no one told you today, please know that you are spectacular!

Day 333: Don't worry. Your glow up is going to be one for the books.

Day 334: Never settle for being someone's back-up plan... You are the blueprint, and never forget that.

Day 335: Love is a powerful feeling. You will not have to wonder if someone loves you. If it is real...you will feel it.

Day 336: You will bounce back. You are resilient. You are strong.

Day 337: One of the most liberating acts of mankind is…apologizing when you are wrong. The only thing better than that is … never repeating what you did to say, "I'm sorry."

Day 338: Do not forget about your elders, especially when they can no longer do the things that they once did. Love them. Support them. Cherish them. For if you are fortunate, you will, one day, be an elder, too.

Day 339: To avoid feeling used in any relationship, you must not give more than you receive. This is not selfish; it is common sense!

Day 340: Model the behavior that you wish to attract.

Day 341: Today will be an awesome day. Claim it.

Day 342: Surround yourself with.... happy people, happy places, happy situations, and keep in your mind...happy thoughts.

Day 343: Help others as much as you can but realize that some people are in need of professional help, and until they get it, they will drain you. Help others but protect yourself.

Day 344: Do not hide your emotions but do learn to control them.

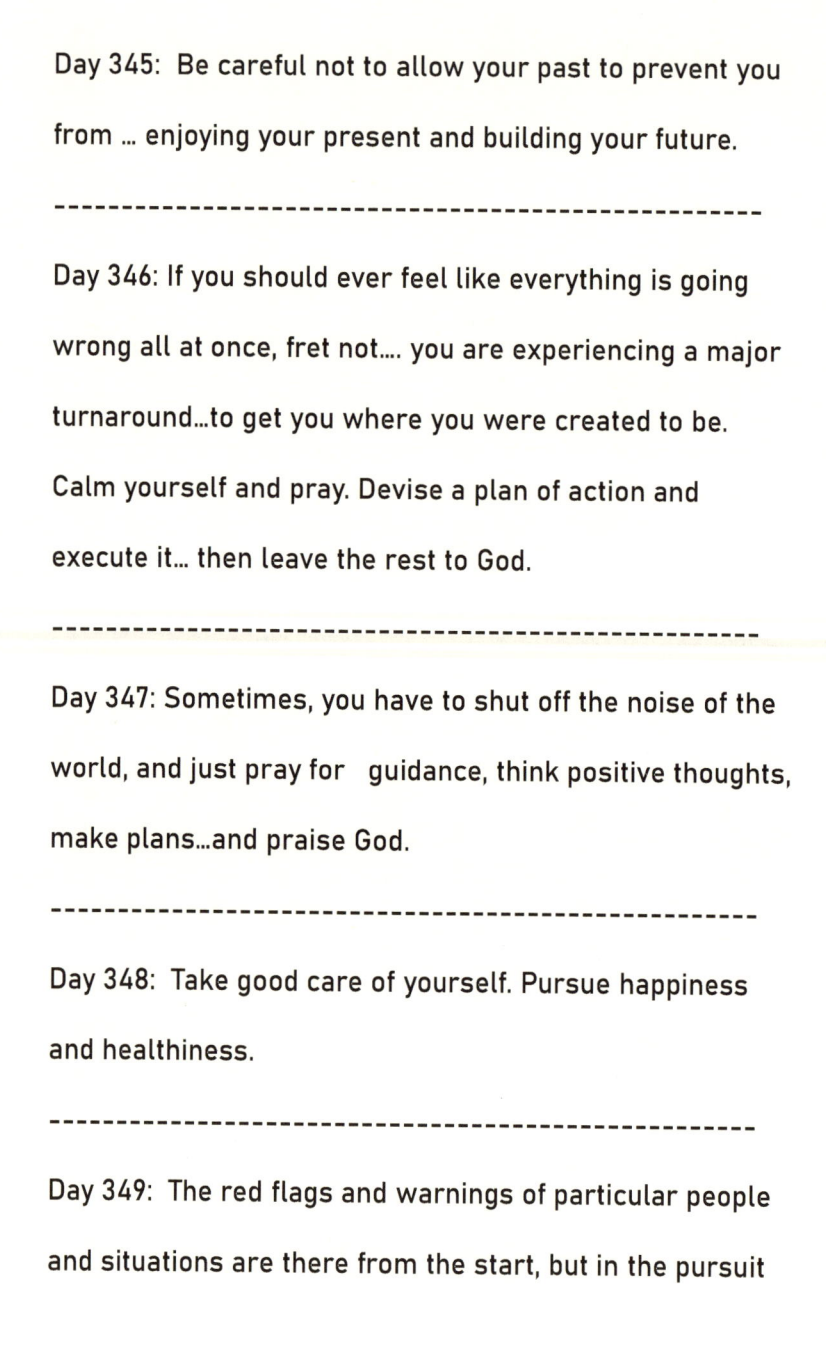

Day 345: Be careful not to allow your past to prevent you from ... enjoying your present and building your future.

Day 346: If you should ever feel like everything is going wrong all at once, fret not.... you are experiencing a major turnaround...to get you where you were created to be. Calm yourself and pray. Devise a plan of action and execute it... then leave the rest to God.

Day 347: Sometimes, you have to shut off the noise of the world, and just pray for guidance, think positive thoughts, make plans...and praise God.

Day 348: Take good care of yourself. Pursue happiness and healthiness.

Day 349: The red flags and warnings of particular people and situations are there from the start, but in the pursuit of happiness, you will sometimes disregard them. Be careful. Stay Watchful. See things for what they are, and do not be blinded by your desires.

Day 350: God has a purpose for your life. You were created for a reason. Tap into the elements of your soul, and live life in purpose and on purpose… fully and completely.

Day 351: There are five seasons on this earth: summer, spring, winter, fall… and your season! This is your season! Claim it!

Day 352: Make time for those people and things that matter in your life. In the process, please do not forget to make time for yourself.

Day 353: At some point, you must forgive yourself, for God has already forgiven you.

Day 354: There are a lot of early mornings… plenty of late nights… and awaking in the wee hours…. associated with success.

Day 355: Enjoy your own company and learn to be content with yourself. If you cannot be happy with yourself, you cannot expect anyone else to be.

Day 356: Sure, traumatic experiences during childhood will be the root cause of many of your issues in life. Use this fact as an agent of change, rather than succumb to playing the blame game. You must let go of past pain in order to set yourself free.

Day 357: Losing a loved one is hard. It is a part of life that is out of human control. Praying to God, grief counseling, and time will allow you to cope with the loss of a loved one. You will also find comfort in knowing that your loved one is alive in spirit and within your heart.

Day 358: Just look at you! After all that you have been through, you are still here. God has a purpose for your life. You are loved. You are "fearfully and wonderfully made." You are a trooper. You were created to do great things. There is no one quite like you, and there never will be! Enjoy this life of yours and make each day purposed-filled.

Day 359: Fake friends and bogus relationships… are a waste of your precious time. Remove fake people and situations from your life, and watch God replace them with meaningful and flourishing connections.

Day 360: Do not retaliate when... someone hurts your feelings, someone breaks your heart, someone betrays you, someone lies on you... Do not retaliate. God feels your pain, and the wicked will feel His wrath. God's children are not to be mistreated!

Day 361: Never devalue yourself for any reason. You are not inferior to anyone or anything. You are amazing. You are worthy. You are blessed beyond measure.

Day 362: Some people will be so quick to count you out... It is not your fault that they can't count. Keep thriving!

Day 363: Detaching yourself from negativity will allow you to attract a wealth of possibilities. Let go of hindrances, and witness elevation on levels... you never even dreamed of.

Day 364: Each day you write your life's story. Make a vow to make it a best seller!

Day 365: When life goes awry, and it is out of your control... When love disappoints and it hurts you to your soul...Know that nothing in life is forever, there will be sunshine and there will be rain. So, you have got to keep on moving, through the laughter and the pain.

Be Blessed

J

References

Guest, Edgar A. "Don't Quit"

The Holy Bible KJV

Tzu, Lao, A Journey of a Thousand"

86

Made in the USA
Columbia, SC
24 December 2024